R00204 00945

CHICAGO PUBLIC LIBRARY
HAROLD WASHINGTON LIBRARY CENTER

R0020400945

YO-AZH-150

cop.1

FORM 125 M

SOCIAL SCIENCES & HISTORY DIVISION

The Chicago Public Library

FEB 2 2 1979

Received

CHICAGO PUBLIC LIBRARY

FOR

REFERENCE USE

ONLY

NOT TO BE TAKEN FROM THIS ROOM

PRACTICAL PUBLIC RELATIONS FOR THE PUBLIC SCHOOLS

by

John Bitter

TROY STATE UNIVERSITY PRESS
TROY, ALABAMA 36081

International Standard Book Number: 0-916624-08-0

Library of Congress Catalog Number: 77-071467

Copyright © 1977 by the Troy State University Press. Printed in the United States of America by the Troy State University Press, Troy, Alabama 36081. No part of this publication may be reproduced or transmitted in any form or by any means electronic or mechanical, including photocopy, recording, or any information storage and retrieval system, without permission in writing from the Troy State University Press.

TABLE OF CONTENTS

LIST OF ILLUSTRATIONS v

Chapter	Page
I.	INTRODUCTION 1

Statement of the Problem
Purpose of the Study

II. PLANNING 5

III. THE AUDIENCE 7

Internal Audience
External Audience

IV. NEWS AND PUBLIC RELATIONS 11

What is News?
Who's Who
Ground Rules
Dissemination
Features
Censorship
Elements of News
Press Releases
Fundamentals of Newswriting
All the Pertinent Facts
Broadcast Releases

V. MEET THE PRESS 35

Eschew Obfuscation
Mechanics of Press Conferences

VI. PHOTO COVERAGE 43

VII. SUMMARY AND CONCLUSIONS 45

APPENDIX 47
Definition of Terms

SELECTED BIBLIOGRAPHY 49

INDEX 57

LIST OF ILLUSTRATIONS

1. News Release Form 21
2. Sample Worksheet 24
3. Sample News Release 28
4. Newspaper Write-Up 29
5. Sample Broadcast Release 30
6. Broadcast Release Time Count 32

Chapter I

INTRODUCTION

Public education in this country has become one of the favorite targets of critics, both within the fraternity and without. The list of grievances against schools, administrators, and teachers seems endless. The roster of accomplishments and positive acts is virtually nil.

In reality, there is perhaps as much good to be said of public education in the United States as there is bad, but this side of the story is seldom heard.

Why is this?

Probably the major factor contributing to this imbalance of information is the public educator's reluctance, or inability to communicate, or a combination of the two.[1]

Over the years the educator has become gun-shy when dealing with the public, and often tends to run from his inquisitors when problems arise. He will often closet himself in an atmosphere of isolationism, believing, perhaps, that no news about public education is good news. This is not true, however, as education crowds national defense and politics for space on the front pages of our newspapers and prominence on radio and television news programs.

Unlike politicians and generals, school administrators, for the most part, have not yet learned how to effectively communicate with the public.

Statement of the Problem

In addressing himself to the problem many legislators have with the education community, Samuel Halperin observes that the greatest stumbling block confounding the educator's efforts is his inability to say what has to be said. In short, educators seem unable to communicate in simple, understandable terms.[2]

In years past, the educator could avoid the public, going about his business with little need or desire to communicate with a public that tended to take his good

PUBLIC RELATIONS

works for granted. However, over the past two decades, the public has developed an increasing awareness of education and its impact on our society. As a consequence, education has become newsworthy[3] and the educator has become a valuable news source.[4] Unfortunately, there are too many educators today who continue to maintain an attitude of indifference — if not outright hostility — toward the public, and the news media.[5] Far too many refuse to take the time, or make the effort, to get acquainted with the various news media and to learn how best to communicate with it.[6]

The superintendent and the central office staff, from the largest of school districts to the smallest, have a herculean administrative task to perform. Theirs is not just a matter of keeping schools open, paying employees, operating school buses, and feeding youngsters; it's complying with state and national regulations, as well as with federal court orders, answering more than a respectable number of questions from parents and concerned citizens, and trying to keep everyone happy — or at least somewhat content.

Invariably, something connected with this routine is going to become newsworthy. The superintendent would like to think that everything he and his system does is of interest to the general public. Unfortunately, this is not always so. The average person tends to take the good for granted. So, too, does the newsman. He expects school to open as scheduled. The fact that there were no racial incidents at the local high school is not normally significant, nor is the fact that the teachers are doing their jobs, the buses are running properly, and the children are learning at what can be considered an acceptable rate.[7] However, when any of these things fails to take place, that's news. That is when the newsman calls the superintendent's office and wants facts, statistics, or statements. And, in too many cases, this is when he does not get them.

If the educator hopes to develop a substantial educational program in his community, he must have the

INTRODUCTION

understanding, cooperation, and support of its citizens.[8] He must rebuild the trust the public once had in its schools, and make the community feel that the public school is its school.[9] He can't run from the facts, no matter how he may dislike them. Since much of a school's success depends upon its relationship with the community, that community must be kept informed as to its accomplishments, purposes, needs, and objectives.[10]

To accomplish this task a school system needs a qualified person assigned to the central office staff to work with the news media. In a recent poll of Alabama public school administrators and lay board members, 69 per cent of those responding felt there was a need for such a specialist on the staff.[11] Unfortunately, however, of Alabama's 127 public school systems, only five are of sufficient size as to warrant this expense, and only four (Birmingham City, Jefferson County, Mobile County, and Huntsville City) employ full-time public relations practitioners.[12]

It has been suggested that a school system of 50,000 student population could justify such a position on the central office staff.[13] Huntsville, incidentally, has an enrollment of only 33,300 students.[14]

We see, then, that in Alabama there are 123 public school systems that either cannot afford, or do not wish to incur the expense of, a full-time practitioner.

Purpose of this Book

It is with the preceding in mind that this publication was prepared. In gathering material for a thesis on the communication gap existing between educators and the news media, and from eight years experience as a newsman with *The Montgomery Advertiser,* it has become clear to this writer that school administrators have difficulty in communicating with members of the news media. In some instances this shortcoming is caused by hostility, but in many cases it is a matter of a lack of knowledge of how to effectively state one's case.

PUBLIC RELATIONS

It is the newsman's task to gather news about public education for presentation to the public. The public supports the schools and, in effect, pays the salaries of those employed within the system. Therefore, that public has a right to know how its tax dollars are being spent.

In general, the newsman does not approach the educator with a hostile attitude. It is only after his attempts to gather information have been met with evasions, obfuscation, and delay does animosity set in.

If the school administrator wishes to maintain public support for the system, it is his responsibility to see that the public is informed of its accomplishments and needs. The degree of public support of the schools depends to a large extent upon how well the administrator articulates his system's educational efforts.

By utilizing the information contained herein, the school administrator, lay board member, principal, or teacher should be able to tell the school story to the public in the most favorable manner.

School officials can expect to have frequent dealings with the news media, and should be prepared to both generate positive news as well as be able to quickly and intelligently respond to queries from the news gatherers.

In this respect, the first thing a school system should do is to establish a public relations policy.

Chapter II

PLANNING

Since public schools are public institutions, supported by public tax dollars, they need the goodwill of this public if they are to survive. Consequently, school boards and administrators must give careful consideration to how they deal with the public — which, in most cases, is through the news media.[1]

Board members and administrators should be aware, however, that public relations is not a panacea for all problems;[2] it is a team effort, an effort which requires the cooperation of the entire staff, from superintendent to janitor, each aware of the system's program, and understanding their part in it.[3]

In establishing its objectives, a school board would do well to include the following:

--Inform the public about the work of its schools.

--Establish public confidence in the schools.

--Rally support for proper maintenance of the educational program.

--Develop public awareness of the importance of education in a democracy.

--Improve the partnership concept by uniting parents and teachers in meeting the educational problems of children.

--To integrate the home, the school, and the community in meeting the needs of the children.

--Correct misunderstandings as to the aims and objectives of the school system.[4]

Once the board has established its plan and has agreed upon its objectives, it should either hire a qualified public relations practitioner — if it is within the system's means — or designate a member of the central office staff as the responsible spokesman. Because of the sensitive nature of this task, the person designated should have direct access to the superintendent since he must be in a position to provide prompt and reliable information to the news media.[5]

PUBLIC RELATIONS

Next the board should address itself to outlining the functions of its public relations effort, which should include the following responsibilities:

--Establish and maintain efficient channels of communication between personnel within the school system.

--Coordinate public relations activities of all persons employed by the board of education.

--Provide services on call which contribute either directly or indirectly to the strengthening of the school/community relations program.

--Work cooperatively with outside groups and organizations that have constructive interests in public education.

--Undertake assigned responsibilities in the school/community relations program.

--Involve lay citizens in the work of the school and in the solving of educational problems.

--Have the person assigned the public relations task serve as a consultant to the superintendent and through him to the board of education on matters involving relations with the community.

--Appraise the effectiveness of the public relations program and make recommendations for its improvement.[6]

Chapter III

THE AUDIENCE

One of the first things the practitioner, the superintendent, and the board must understand is that there are two audiences to be reached in their public relations effort: internal and external.

Internal Audience

All too often public relations efforts founder because only half the audience is reached. Management tends to take for granted its employees, their families and friends in its effort to sway outside public opinion. Rapport between the school hierarchy and the classroom teachers is every bit as important as the opinions held by groups outside the school.[1]

For the public relations program to be successful, all employees of the system must feel that they are an integral part of the team, understand their function in the successful operation of the system, and possess a sense of pride and dignity in their job.

The most effective spokesman for an organization is the individual worker. His remarks and opinions about his job expressed in the community do more to help form public attitudes about the system than any amount of flowery news releases prepared by journalistic wordsmiths.

Only through a system of two-way communication can the members of the organization feel they are essential and respected cogs in the corporate wheel.

They need to know what is being done within the system and why.

Any number of devices are available to provide internal information flow, from in-house newspapers, to internal memoranda. Mainly, the size of the system dictates the sophistication of the effort to be put into play.

In a system of a few hundred employees, word of mouth may be one of the most effective means of getting the message to the staff. Whatever the device used, it must be honest and thorough. The employee, as well as the

PUBLIC RELATIONS

public, is quick to detect a phony act and can be expected to react adversely.

External Audience

The external audience is generally reached through the various communication media. But even here some systems reach only a fraction of the potential audience.

In order for the system to effectively bring its message to the people it must employ all facets of the news media. In preparing news releases for public dissemination, the practitioner must understand that there are more avenues open to him than merely the local daily newspaper.[2] Consider, for example, Montgomery, Alabama. In addition to the morning *Montgomery Advertiser,* there is also the *Alabama Journal,* published by the same company but appearing in the afternoon. In addition, both the Associated Press and United Press International maintain bureaus in the capital city. There is also the weekly *Montgomery Independent,* the *Alabama News Magazine,* plus 11 radio stations and three television stations.[3] In addition, there are alumni bulletins at all of the colleges and universities in town, and the list of professional and trade organizations putting out periodic publications includes: *The Air University Review, Alabama Builder, Alabama Cattleman, Alabama Conservation, Alabama Farm Bureau News, Alabama Food Merchants Journal, Alabama Forest Products, Alabama Librarian, Alabama LP Gas News, Alabama Municipal Journal, Alabama School Journal, Alabama Trucker, AREA Magazine, Coach and Athlete, Journal of the Medical Association of Alabama, Loggin' Times, Pulpwood Products and Saw Mill Logging,* and probably a good many more.[4] Each of these publications should be considered as a potential outlet for news releases prepared by the practitioner.

For example, should a student in the school system attain some high scholastic honor it would be of interest to the local daily newspapers, probably the weekly newspaper, perhaps regional magazines, the local television

THE AUDIENCE

stations and radio stations in the area.

But this is not the end. How about the parents' home towns? The grandparents would like to know that their grandchild is bringing fame to the family; therefore local papers there should be considered in mailing releases. Also the local broadcasters should not be overlooked. Then there's the place of employment of the parents. Should their company publish an internal periodical, it may well be interested in how the offspring of its workers are doing.

Alumni bulletins could be another source, as well as professional and fraternal publications and bulletins and civic club news letters. The potential is virtually endless. In most cases, it is limited only by the imagination of the practitioner.

The system may find it a wise investment to purchase a copy of *Ayer's Directory of Publications,* published by Ayer Press, Philadelphia, Pennsylvania, *Editor and Publisher Year Book,* put out by Editor and Publisher, 850 Third Avenue, New York, local news media directories, often published by a special interest group in the area, any almanac for a listing of colleges and universities, telephone directories for listings of associations and civic organizations, and chamber of commerce listings of groups and organizations. Many of these aids are also available in the reference section of the local library.

Chapter IV

NEWS AND PUBLIC RELATIONS

Before venturing forth into medialand, the novice practitioner should equip himself with some basic philosophies and guidelines. The first of these should be: "A good press comes from good press relations, which are, in effect, good human relations."[1] Remember that editors and broadcasters work on deadlines, that they are people — individuals who have feelings, opinions, likes and dislikes. This is one of the reasons so many successful public relations practitioners across the land are former newsmen — they know the profession, they know what is wanted and what is not wanted.[2]

Probably the best advice for public relations people was given by Thomas Clark of the Des Moines (Iowa) *Register and Tribune*, who said: "If you have a story to tell, get all the facts and don't worry about the writing — we'll rewrite anyway. If you don't have a story, keep quiet and save the postage."[3]

What Is News?

What far too many practitioners — both in education as well as business and industry — fail to realize is that there is little that is newsworthy about the ongoing program. Education, like everything else in life, becomes newsworthy when attempts are made to change or improve it.[4]

Which brings up the question: What, then, is news?

In 1932, the late Willard G. Bleyer defined news as:

> ...anything timely that is interesting and significant to readers in respect to their personal affairs or their relation to society, and the best news is that which possesses the greatest degree of this interest and significance for the greatest number.[5]

In his textbook, *The Professional Journalist*, John A. Hohenberg provides a number of definitions of news.

PUBLIC RELATIONS

He quotes Dean Lyle M. Spencer of the University of Washington as describing it as:

...any event, idea, or opinion that is timely, that interests or affects a large number of persons in a community, and that is capable of being understood by them.[6]

Mitchell V. Charnley adds to these sentiments by saying: "News is the timely reporting of facts or opinions of either interest or importance, or both, to a considerable number of people."[7]

He goes on to add that:

News is tomorrow's history done up in today's neat package...(it) is the fuel that keeps the wheels of modern civilization turning...(and it) is the timely, concise, accurate report of an event; it is not the event itself.[8]

Like the sound of the tree falling in an empty forest, news is not news until it is reported. From the standpoint of the public relations practitioner, then, his news is not news until he gets it to the media. And even then, it is not news unless it is newsworthy.

There are four major characteristics of news that should serve as the practitioner's guide in determining if what he plans to say is worth saying. These are: accuracy, interest, timeliness, and explanation.[9] If none of these characteristics are present, the practitioner may wish to reassess his effort. In this regard, Alexander B. Adams provides a few comments on what is not news. Primarily, it is not something created by the public relations person in an effort to get the superintendent's name in headlines.

It is often difficult to tell the superintendent that his pet project is not newsworthy. It is easier to give in and grind out a piece of useless drivel rather than argue with the boss. Yet, while this may help the practitioner with respect to remaining within the good graces of the superintendent, it can seriously harm his reputation as a news source.[10]

NEWS AND PUBLIC RELATIONS

Who's Who

If the school system wishes to enjoy amicable relations with the news media, it must endeavor to meet the newsman half way. While the reporter is expected to quickly learn the intricacies of education, the school systems, the various federal programs, and the educational hierarchy, few educators take the time to understand the workings of the local newspapers and broadcast stations.[11]

The member of the central office staff entrusted with the system's public relations responsibility should attempt to acquaint himself with the operations of the local media, its peculiar demands, and its management structure.

In most cases, a weekly newspaper operates with an extremely small staff. News releases sent to "The Editor" will most likely reach the person interested in them.

On larger papers, certain reporters often handle specific news "beats," such as education. School news releases should be sent to the "Education Editor," or to the staff writer by name, if the practitioner is certain that this person is, in fact, handling educational news. If in doubt, address news releases to the "City Editor."

Simply addressing releases to "The Editor" of daily newspapers can cause unnecessary delays since there are a number of editors on the staff, any one of whom could receive the release. If it does not reach the right editor, it could be passed about through distribution channels, losing a day or two en route.

At radio stations, releases sent to the "News Director" are likely to fall into the right hands since many stations often have only one person handling news.

Much the same is true of television, where the News Director assigns the various newsmen to cover specific areas and events, and he controls the news input and flow.

For the wire services, Associated Press and United Press International, press releases addressed to the "Bureau Chief" will reach the correct person.

The new practitioner may do well to make a courtesy call to the various media in his city, taking particular care

PUBLIC RELATIONS

to time his visit when the paper or broadcast station is not approaching deadline or air time.

After this initial visit, unless he has a perishable item that needs immediate delivery, his absence will be welcome.

Ground Rules

In dealing with the various media, there are a few rules that should be observed if one is to enjoy a fruitful relationship. The most important of these concerns the sword that hangs over every newsman's head: deadline.

For the reporters' material to be published or aired, they must complete their writing by a certain, virtually inflexible time. Consequently, when a reporter calls the school system seeking information, the practitioner should either provide the material at once or, if it is necessary to obtain it from another source, or seek additional facts, the newsman should be asked when the information is needed, and then be provided with it promptly. Giving the information five minutes late is the same as giving it a day late.

Additionally, when the material is provided to the media it should be factual, in usable form and not clouded with qualifications, reservations, and obfuscations. In addition, it should be based on sound authority.[12]

The reporter, in gathering his news, expects no favors from the practitioner; rather, all he asks is fair and impartial treatment. He expects to be told what the story is, when it will break, and be given a chance to interview the central figures involved.

If the story is routine, don't attempt to glamorize it by concocting some aura of urgency. The newsman will resent your using his valuable time to travel miles to pick up a handout that could have been mailed.[13]

Each of the various media observes different deadlines. Each particular station or newspaper may have deadlines different from others. The practitioner should ascertain the exact time of these deadlines and respect them. No

NEWS AND PUBLIC RELATIONS

newsman appreciates having a public relations person hovering about, trying to peddle his news releases while the eleventh hour draws near with agonizing speed.

In addition to observing deadlines, public relations persons should gear the release of hard news items so as not to favor any one segment of the media.

For example: National Merit Scholarship Foundation news releases are embargoed so that one year the morning papers are first to print the winners; the next year the favor goes to the afternoon papers.

In the same vein, exclusives should be handled judiciously. Straight news stories should be released to all the media at one time. On the other hand, if an enterprising reporter digs up something on his own, his enterprise might be rewarded by delaying release of the information to the other media until after his story appears.[14]

Providing newsmen with "off the record" information should be given serious consideration before remarks are made. Many reporters do not like to receive information with restrictions tied to it. If they listen to "off the record" remarks from one source, and then learn of the same information from another — without qualification — they are put on the spot. They must either withhold information they have learned, or release it and appear to have violated a confidence.[15] It might be added that it is considered dirty pool for a spokesman to render remarks and then follow them with the admonition: "This is off the record, of course." Most newsmen feel that anything uttered prior to the qualifying remark is fair game.

Dissemination

What is news to some is not necessarily news to all. Nevertheless, some practitioners insist on "shotgunning" their releases to the entire media, hoping that out of their barrage someone is liable to use something.[16] After a while, recipients of habitual shotgunners' materials often

PUBLIC RELATIONS

throw away the entire press packet after a cursory glance at the return address.[17]

Another dangerous device is to send copies of a news release to four or five different people on a newspaper, assuming that the chances of it being used will be multiplied. This theory has two potential pitfalls: the first being that the item may appear twice in the same paper because two reporters turned in the same rewrite. This causes the newspaper embarrassment and could adversely affect future dealing. The second time around, each of the recipients may assume that someone else will handle it and no one turns it in. The result: no coverage at all. One release to each of the media is sufficient.

Features

Quite often practitioners discover some interesting aspect of their system that would make a good feature story. Most newsmen welcome good feature material. They appreciate all the help the practitioner may provide, such as stock photographs, fact sheets, background material, statistics. But they prefer to write the story themselves.[18]

Censorship

The easiest way to get on the wrong side of a newsman is to demand to see his copy prior to its use. Some reporters, out of a desire to assure accuracy, may show the practitioner their notes, but they will resent someone asking to see them for final approval. The reporter does not work for the school system; he owes it nothing more than any other segment of society he may be assigned to report upon.[19]

Above all, never ask a reporter to suppress a story. A reporter has three principal duties: to report the news accurately, to protect his sources of information, and to respect such confidences as he is willing to accept. His loyalty is to his publisher or employer, and to no one else.[20]

NEWS AND PUBLIC RELATIONS

Elements of News

Much of what holds true for news reporting holds equally true for news release writing. There's nothing newsworthy about the daily routine. Therefore, a news release should be of substance. Does what you intend to write about have an impact upon the daily lives of the general public?

A major element of news is IMMEDIACY. Last week's happenings are history. The public wants to know what took place today, or what will occur tomorrow.

Readers and listeners, as well as viewers, are interested in what is taking place in the schools in their area. The PROXIMITY of the news is important. A court-ordered integration plan in Boston, Massachusetts is interesting. But one for the local system is news.

Which brings about the next element, that of CONSEQUENCE. What effect will this news item have on the lives of the students and their families in your school district?

CONFLICT always makes news, although many school people tend to attempt to avoid it whenever possible. However, the public wants to know what happened and why when tempers flare up.

Another element of news is ODDITY. This is an element that can get one into difficulty if not handled with care. The strange and unusual will get attention, but exploiting oddity can lead one down the road to cheap press-agentry.

Another element that requires special handling is SEX. While there is always a certain amount of news interest in sex, these three letters can cause headaches. Sex, while newsworthy, must be handled judiciously.

EMOTION is an important news element and includes love, hate, happiness, sadness, anger, sympathy, ambition, envy, generosity, humor, and tragedy.

While PROMINENCE is another important element of news, the practitioner is well advised not to attempt to overpower the press with the prominence of his superintendent and deluge the media with news releases

PUBLIC RELATIONS

concerning every ribbon-cutting and school lunchroom visit made by the superintendent. Likewise, it is a bad practice to single out certain students for press exposure because of their family or their academic superiority. Oftentimes, a student who is not doing too well, or may be losing interest in school, may be directed back on course through his having had his picture in the paper in connection with some school activity.

SUSPENSE is more apt to be found in feature stories than in most news releases, since a feature must build up to a suspenseful climax. Should the practitioner attempt this sort of thing in a straight news story, he might find his climax missing as the story is cut to fill available space.

One element that is always a sure-fire item for school news releases is anything reporting PROGRESS. In this age of dissatisfaction and disillusionment over the nation's educational efforts, progress could, to paraphrase General Electric, be education's most important product.[21]

In working with any of these elements of news, the practitioner should be advised to follow these simple rules:

BE BRIEF. Say what needs to be said, then end the release.

BE CLEAR. Avoid jargon and educational terminology. Assume that the reader knows nothing about the subject and write in such a way that when he finishes reading it he will know as much about it as the writer.

BE COHERENT. Move smoothly from one point to the next. Don't skip about. Outline your news release before you write it.

UNIFY. Don't attempt to incorporate the sum of human knowledge in one release. If you have a multitude of subjects to cover, devote a separate release to each.

EMPHASIZE YOUR POINT. Make sure the reader understands the point intended to be made. The best way to do this is to place the subject of emphasis in the lead paragraph of the news release.

BE OBJECTIVE. Don't try to slant news releases in such a manner as they become publicity puffs. Tell the truth — both sides of the story.[22]

NEWS AND PUBLIC RELATIONS

Press Releases

The press release has as its purpose the conveyance of a message to the widest possible public in the clearest manner, a message that should leave a favorable image of the organization in the minds of its audience.

While there are certain basic elements to a good news release, there are also certain elements that must be included in the format of the release form itself.

The news release, whether it is prepared on expensive letterhead forms, or typed on plain bond paper, must inform its recipient of its origin. Both the name, address and telephone number of the organization should appear at the top of the form, also the name of the responsible person who should be called for any additional information. That person's home phone number should also be included.

Next there should appear a release date, in order that the recipient may know when the material may be published or broadcast. Normally a release will contain the note: "FOR IMMEDIATE RELEASE," indicating that it may be used at any time after receipt. However, there will be times when the organization may want to have the material in the hands of the media, but not have it released until after a certain time. Embargoes, as they are called, should be used sparingly, and should never be used as an effort to control the timing of news. The practitioner must understand that an embargo in no way commits an editor, and some have been known to openly break embargoes as a form of protest.[23] If a release date is necessary, a notation should appear at the top of the release. For example:

FOR RELEASE AFTER NOON, APRIL 14

Since some newspapers may wish to use the news release as received, with appropriate editorial notations, the originator should leave considerable blank space between the heading and release information and the actual text of the news release.

The text should begin with a "dateline" which identifies

PUBLIC RELATIONS

the locale of the event. It also includes, in parenthesis, the date the information is released. Following this information is the actual news release itself, prepared in journalistic style.

If the release consumes more than one page, end each page with the word "more" enclosed in parenthesis. This tells the editor that there is additional material to follow.

On succeeding pages, in the upper left-hand corner, type the words "ADD-TWO," or the numerical notation, "2-2-2," and a word or two to identify the story. If a release were to concern the hiring of new teachers, the notation on the second page might be: "ADD-TWO-HIRING." If the release continues to a third page, the notation would be: "ADD-THREE-HIRING," and so on for as many pages as are used.

In preparing the news release, the practitioner should never use more than one side of the paper, and all copy should be double spaced.

At the end of the release, a number of options are available to signal the conclusion of the copy. Some professionals will end their releases with the word "end," others with the numerals "30," and still others with the symbols " ### ," all of which tell the editor that the story has ended. (For examples of format cited above, see figure 1.)

Fundamentals of News Writing

One of the reasons many newsmen are recruited for public relations work is that they have experience in news writing. It stands to reason that if a school system wants something to get into the newspaper – or on the air – it should be written in the style of that particular medium.[24]

School officials should understand and respect the fact that the news media employ a different manner of writing than is taught in the English classroom. There is a tendency on the part of some school people to use the redundancies and jargon that are a part of their life when attempting to communicate with the media. In so doing,

NEWS AND PUBLIC RELATIONS

Figure 1

NEWS RELEASE FORM

YOURTOWN INDEPENDENT SCHOOL DISTRICT
1234 Smith Street
Yourtown, Alabama 33333

    (Give complete address)

For additional information contact:
       Joe Smith   222-1111 (Office)
                      221-3333 (Home)

(Identify source and include telephone numbers where he may be reached)

FOR IMMEDIATE RELEASE (May be used upon receipt)

                        (or)

ADVANCE RELEASE FOR SEPTEMBER 15, 1976 (Embargo)

   YOURTOWN, Ala. (Sept. 15, 1976) — (dateline)

                       (more)   (indicates release is continued on succeeding page, or pages)

                       ###
                       -30-   (each of these symbols indicates end of the release)
                       end

PUBLIC RELATIONS

they often insist upon dispatching clumsy, lengthy tomes when a concise, well-written release is needed. As a result, their efforts are frequently in vain.

In essence, good news release writing is good news writing. A press release should be written in much the same manner as a news item in the daily paper.

The style of the news release should depend upon the recipient, but in all cases it should be terse, factual and contain certain specific information, the WHO, WHAT, WHEN, WHERE, WHY, and HOW of a story.

In most cases, newspapers follow the Associated Press style format. Some have their own style of news writing and have published manuals for their reporters. If possible, the practitioner should obtain a copy of the accepted stylebook and follow it when preparing news releases. If this is not possible, read the local newspaper and see how local news stories are written, then follow that example.[25]

In preparing news releases involving children, certain information should always be included, such as: the child's full name, not nicknames; his school grade level; his age; home address; and names of parents.

When releasing information concerning staff and faculty members where the names of schools they have attended is used, always include the city and state in which the school is located.

Generally, the age of male adults is given, but the ladies are afforded the courtesy of omitting this information.

When referring to schools, specify if they are elementary, junior high, middle, or high schools.

Additionally, there are certain news writing rules that apply to all fields, foremost among these is: write tight. Omit unnecessary words. Don't write "6 o'clock Thursday evening the 21st of June." Standard usage is: "6 p.m., June 21."

Use short paragraphs. Write for the eye. A paragraph of four or five typewritten lines is about average.

NEWS AND PUBLIC RELATIONS

All The Pertinent Facts

As an exaggerated example of how much supporting data must, of necessity, go into a news release and a news story, take the rhyme "Jack and Jill". Here's how it might be written as a news item:

JACK Nurdlinger, 13, son of Mr. and Mrs. Seymour B. Nurdlinger of 3132 Pfister Lane, Centerville, a student at Central High School, *AND JILL* Schwartzloiter, 13, daughter of Mr. and Mrs. R. C. Schwartzloiter, 4141 Crapotnik Drive, also a Central High student, *WENT UP A HILL* located in the southeastern section of the city Friday *TO FETCH A PAIL OF WATER,* local authorities said.

JACK FELL DOWN AND BROKE HIS CROWN, police said in their preliminary report of the incident. However, officials at Mercy Hospital declined to comment on the extent of the injuries or on the boy's status other than that "he is resting comfortably and is in satisfactory condition."

Police officers disclosed that at the time of Jack's fall, *JILL CAME TUMBLING AFTER,* but were unable to state whether she had been injured.

An ambulance attendant said that both children had been taken to the hospital emergency room but that he did not know if the girl had been admitted. Hospital officials report she had been treated for minor injuries and released.

These are the facts the newsman needs in order to write a news story. He can't guess at the details, or suppose that such and such took place. The practitioner must provide him with as much complete and accurate information as possible.

All too often it is said that newsmen never get anything right. In most instances, if they have complete information they will present a true and accurate chronicle of events.

It is the PR practitioner's task to see that this information is furnished promptly and accurately.

In writing the news release, answer these six basic and

PUBLIC RELATIONS

essential questions:
- Who did it?
- What did they do?
- When did they do it?
- Why was it done?
- Where was it done?
- How was it done?

Figure 2

SAMPLE WORK SHEET

WHO _____

_____

WHAT _____

_____

WHEN _____

_____

WHERE _____

_____

WHY _____

_____

HOW _____

_____

_____

_____

NEWS AND PUBLIC RELATIONS

A worksheet, as shown in figure 2, is handy when beginning to gather information for a news release. If the questions listed are properly answered, the news release writes itself.

The first paragraph of a news release is often the most difficult to write. The lead paragraph must contain a good number of the answers to the six basic questions listed above, yet it must be concise and interesting enough to catch and hold the reader's attention. It need not be a literary monument – there's no room for flowery phraseology. The lead paragraph, as well as the remainder of the release, should contain, in brief form, as much information as possible.

This is often difficult when dealing with bureaucracies. Individuals tend to have lengthy titles, compounded by the fact that the division of the organization for which they work also tends to lean towards lengthy nomenclatures.

A news release concerning a hypothetical Dr. Sam Smith, deputy assistant coordinator of adult evening programs for the Department of Vocational and Technical Education of Yourtown Independent School District, presents the practitioner with a healthy challenge as he addresses himself to writing the lead paragraph. The WHO could consume an entire paragraph in itself. Yet it is mandatory that Dr. Smith be identified in full, cumbersome though this may be.

In order to avoid such a problem, the writer may want to open his news release with a phrase such as:

"The head of the Yourtown School District's adult evening program, Dr. Sam Smith, . . ." His complete title could be picked up in a succeeding paragraph with a comment such as: "In his capacity as deputy . . . Smith . . ." There are ways to get around the problem.

In arranging the facts of his story, the practitioner should follow the principle of the inverted pyramid. Begin the release with the most important facts: the climactic lead. Then follow with additional pertinent facts, followed in a descending order of importance, secondary and

PUBLIC RELATIONS

tertiary facts and then "nice to know" information.

Rarely will all the information contained in a news release be printed in the newspaper or be read over the air. Editors will cut a news release from the bottom up, until it fits the amount of space or time available. The editor does not have time to ponder what is important in the release and what can be eliminated. He merely begins chopping with the last paragraph and moves up until he has a fit.

As an example of how a typical news release might be written, a hypothetical Superintendent Frick Frack of Yourtown Independent School District, calls his administrative assistant into his office and tells him he wants the following news item publicized:

The school system has received a $567,321 grant from the U.S. Department of Health, Education, and Welfare under Title III of the Elementary and Secondary Education Act of 1965, to launch a public relations program in the school system.

A program coordinator will be hired at a salary of $18,000 a year. He will occupy office space in the Board of Education building and will have a secretary, also paid from the grant.

The grant is for three years. Its purpose is to establish a public and community relations program for the district.

Each of the system's 55 schools will designate a "correspondent" to furnish newsworthy items to the PR man who will then disseminate to the local media such materials and other items he feels are of sufficient import to be considered newsworthy.

The PR coordinator will prepare a public relations plan for the system as well as handbooks for the individual correspondents.

Prior to the beginning of the school year, a workshop will be held at U.S. Grant High School for board members, "correspondents," central office staff, and principals.

A second, week-long workshop will be held October 25 to 29 at Grant High School for the "correspondents" and principals who will outline a program and will be counseled on public and community relations principles

NEWS AND PUBLIC RELATIONS

and news writing techniques.

In addition, a system-wide newspaper will be prepared, its purpose being to reach all professional and non-professional staff members, to publicize their accomplishments, provide pertinent professional information from the central office, and present current items of interest.

Before preparing the news release, the administrative assistant might want to prepare a rough outline of pertinent facts gathered in his talk with the superintendent. He might employ a worksheet as described in figure 2, answering the six pertinent questions.

First, he wants to know WHO.

In this case it is the school system. It is not Superintendent Frack. He merely conveys the message.

The WHAT is the $567,321 HEW grant.

The WHEN would be "today."

The system's 55 schools are the WHERE, and the HOW would be through Title III of ESEA.

The WHY would be to launch a public relations program for the school system.

With this basic information the practitioner can set about writing his release, as shown in figure 3.

Figure 4 is an example of how the local newspaper might treat the same news release upon its receipt. Note that many of the details, such as the exact amount of the grant, the fact that it was under Title III, and other tertiary facts were omitted from the news story. For most readers, "HEW," or even "a federal grant," would be sufficient background information. Also note that the news item information is in much the same order as that contained in the news release.

A second release, figure 5, could be prepared for the broadcast media, providing the information in readily usable form. It would be wise, however, to include a copy of the press release with the broadcast format when sending the material to broadcasters.

PUBLIC RELATIONS

Figure 3

SAMPLE NEWS RELEASE

YOURTOWN INDEPENDENT SCHOOL SYSTEM
1234 Smith Street
Yourtown, Alabama 33333

For additional information contact:
        Joe Smith   222-1111 (Office)
                          221-3333 (Home)

FOR IMMEDIATE RELEASE

YOURTOWN, Ala. (Oct. 3, 1976) – Yourtown Independent Schools received a $567,321 grant from the U.S. Department of Health, Education, and Welfare today to launch a public relations program in the system's 55 schools.

Superintendent Frick Frack said the program will be funded through Title III of the Elementary and Secondary Education Act of 1965 for three years.

The system will employ a project coordinator to supervise the program, conduct workshops and be responsible for the preparation of news releases for the news media.

A workshop will be held at U.S. Grant High School Oct. 25 to 29 for teacher "correspondents" and principals from each of the schools.

Frack said the system also will publish a monthly newspaper for faculty and staff containing professional news items, departmental policy notices and information concerning accomplishments of members of the system.

NEWS AND PUBLIC RELATIONS

Figure 4

NEWSPAPER WRITE-UP

YOURTOWN SCHOOLS GET FEDERAL CASH FOR PUBLIC RELATIONS PROGRAM

Yourtown Independent Schools today received $500,000 from HEW to launch a public relations program in the 55 public schools here.

Superintendent Frick Frack said the system will hire a project coordinator to oversee the three year project which will involve disseminating news releases to the media as well as publishing an in-house newspaper for members of the system.

A workshop for teacher "correspondents" and principals will be held Oct. 25 to 29 at U.S. Grant High School, said Frack.

PUBLIC RELATIONS

Figure 5

SAMPLE BROADCAST RELEASE

YOURTOWN INDEPENDENT SCHOOL SYSTEM
1234 Smith Street
Yourtown, Alabama 33333

For additional information contact:
    Joe Smith   222-1111 (Office)
                        221-3333 (Home)

October 3, 1976

FOR IMMEDIATE RELEASE

15 lines

NEWSCASTER: YOURTOWN PUBLIC SCHOOLS TODAY RECEIVED A $567,321 GRANT FROM HEW TO LAUNCH A COMMUNITY AND PUBLIC RELATIONS PROGRAM. SUPERINTENDENT FRICK FRACK SAID THE SYSTEM WILL HIRE A COORDINATOR TO SUPERVISE ACTIVITIES FOR THE SYSTEM'S 55 SCHOOLS. A WEEK-LONG WORKSHOP FOR TEACHER CORRESPONDENTS AND PRINCIPALS WILL BE HELD AT U.S. GRANT HIGH SCHOOL BEGINNING OCTOBER 25.

#####

NEWS AND PUBLIC RELATIONS

Broadcast Releases

In preparing press releases, the staff member entrusted with this task should understand that in addition to daily and weekly newspapers, plus other print publications and the wire services, there are numerous broadcast stations that may well be interested in activities of school systems, individual schools, students, teachers, and others involved in public education.

There are two methods of reaching the broadcasters. The practitioner may send a copy of his regular news release to each station in his area of concern; or, he may want to prepare separate broadcast releases.

It is not absolutely necessary that this be done; in fact, it is more difficult to write for the electronic media than for newspapers. However, it is a means of doubling one's chances of having his news items aired.

If the practitioner chooses to prepare separate broadcast releases, there are a few special rules and precautions he should observe.

First, if there's any way a word can be mispronounced, it most probably will be. In this respect, give the announcer every consideration. Unusual names should be spelled out phonetically in parenthesis immediately after the word along with any other pertinent information, such as underlining the syllable to be emphasized, rhyming clues, or any other aids that will assist in the proper reading and pronunciation. For example:

SUPERINTENDENT JOHN KOHLMAN (*COAL*-MAN) WILL VISIT MUNICH (*MEW*-NICK), GERMANY AND VERSAILLES (VER-*SIGH*), FRANCE. HE WILL BE ACCOMPANIED BY ASSISTANT SUPERINTENDENT JOHN BLOUGH (RHYMES WITH HOW).

Never divide a word at the end of a line. It makes the copy difficult to read. Also, don't split sentences between pages of news copy.

On broadcast releases, note the line count on the upper right hand corner of the page. This tells the announcer

PUBLIC RELATIONS

how long it will take to read. Newscasters read at an average speed of about 15 lines, or 150 words, per minute.

In order to insure accuracy in preparation of news copy, set typewriter margins so as to permit a 70-space line. Figure 6, below, provides a general rule that should be followed in measuring broadcast copy.

Figure 6

BROADCAST RELEASE TIME COUNT

BROADCAST TIME	NUMBER OF TYPED LINES
60 seconds	14 to 16
45 seconds	11 to 12
30 seconds	7 to 8

In writing broadcast releases, the practitioner should remember that they will be read aloud. Write as you would talk. Make sentences brief but complete, averaging about 17 words, but never exceeding 25 words. Use this rule when preparing a broadcast release: Read it aloud. If it is necessary to stop for breath in midsentence, so, too, must the person who will have to read it on the air. Look for a place at this point to end the sentence and begin anew.

In constructing sentences, it is best to use present tense, active verbs. However, one must use common sense. It is not necessary to labor the point, and every news story need not sound as if it had just happened. The active voice does tend to provide for faster pace and clarity, when it is comfortably used.

For example: "The school board met today to discuss teacher salaries and textbooks." (active)

"A meeting of the school board was held today at which time the board members discussed the salary scale for teachers and reviewed textbook materials used in the classrooms." (passive)

Both sentences essentially say the same thing. However, the second sentence is cumbersome, lengthy, and passive.

NEWS AND PUBLIC RELATIONS

A few additional rules to remember when preparing broadcast releases are:

--Avoid beginning with a question.

--Be careful of modifiers. As an example of what could happen with a misplaced modifier, assume a news item was aired stating that: "The secretary to School Superintendent Frick Frack was arrested today for drunk driving."

The listener tuning in late might hear only: " . . .School Superintendent Frick Frack was arrested today for drunk driving."

--Titles should precede names in order to motivate attention.

--Broadcast releases are typed in upper case.

--Some punctuation marks have different meanings in broadcast copy. For example, elipses are used to indicate a pause, or for dramatic effect. They do not fill the same function as intended in normal writing. Material in parenthesis is normally not meant to be read aloud. In broadcast writing, dashes serve the same function as parenthesis in regular news writing.

--Contractions should be used as frequently as possible, in that they read smoothly and add to the conversational tone.

--Avoid the use of "not" in broadcast copy. Use dishonest rather than not honest, innocent in preference to not guilty. A "not" inadvertently dropped changes the entire meaning. Also, a listener may not hear the "not" or be unsure is he had heard it or not. Avoid the possibility of confusion.

--Beware of alliterations, such as "Six students skipped school." An announcer could have a difficult time with such a statement.

--Watch out for homonyms. The ear can't tell the difference between bear and bare, won and one, or meat and meet.[26]

In many cases, the public relations person will be dealing with the broadcast media by phone, announcing an event that is to take place and inviting coverage of it.

PUBLIC RELATIONS

Because of its limited manpower, however, a particular station may wish only to broadcast the announcement. In addition, the news director may ask the practitioner to read his announcement over the phone for immediate transcription. With this in mind, the person calling the station should be prepared to read his release in broadcast style. This requires advance preparation.

First, the practitioner should have the release written in broadcast style.

Second, he should practice reading it before calling the station. When he is suddenly switched over to the station's taping device, he is ready to read the release in a professional manner.

Chapter V

MEET THE PRESS

From time to time school officials may be called upon to conduct press conferences or be the subject of interviews. In this regard, a word of warning: Never call a press conference unless you have something to say. For example: To call a news conference to announce that schools will open as usual could be humiliating when no one shows up, and it could damage credibility and create hostility when the press learns that it has mustered its ranks for naught.

On the other hand, a press conference would be in order to announce that because of the Legislature's failure to pass an appropriation, schools will close by November 1.

Once it has been decided that the news to be released is of sufficient import to warrant a press conference, the next matter to consider is that of who will address the media. If the superintendent does not handle himself well in such instances, someone in the administration of sufficient stature as to be accepted by the press as a reliable spokesman, and who has the ability to articulate, should be selected.

In addressing the media, the person speaking should assume a business-like attitude about the matter. He should avoid conveying the attitude he is all-knowing, and should, as well, refrain from trying to appear contrite and overly humble. Newsmen deal with "spokesmen" on a daily basis. They can spot a phony within seconds, and tend to be merciless with pompous, arrogant bureaucrats.

Prior to conducting the conference or interview, it is wise to consider that those waiting to beard the official at the press table have done their homework. It should follow, then, that the spokesman should prepare himself as well. Facts and statistics should be readily available. The person conducting the news conference, and his staff, should prepare in advance for questions that might be asked. All manner of inquiries should be prepared for. It's better to end the conference or interview with answers unquestioned than the reverse.

PUBLIC RELATIONS

Once the press conference or interview gets underway, remember that those asking the questions speak only standard English. Don't resort to in-house terminology, educationese, or flowery phrases that tend to confuse rather than enlighten.

In addressing oneself to problems involving the school, or school system, approach them from the standpoint of what's best for the public interest, not what's best for the system.

Begin interviews with the most important facts with which you intend to deal. Reporters are looking for a good lead, something that will attract reader or listener attention. Don't save the best for last. There may be someone who has to leave – or falls asleep – before the main point is reached.

If there are some matters that should not be discussed, don't bring them up. Off the record remarks can be disastrous. The spokesman has no obligation to rattle corporate skeletons before the press. If the press wants to uncover them, that's its business. However, once an investigative reporter has uncovered the buried bodies, don't try to lie out of it. No matter how it may hurt, the only recourse is to be as candid as possible.

Should the press conference or interview take an uncomfortable turn, don't lose your composure. Don't argue with the press. Remember this: The press always has the last word. Be tactful and honest; then go home and kick the dog.

Watch for loaded questions based on dubious "facts." A reporter may intend to trap the spokesman with a "when did you stop beating your wife" type of question. Don't repeat the question and don't become defensive. Restate the matter in your own terms and from your own point of view.

A reporter's direct questions deserve an answer, not an evasion. Too many educators offer to tell the reporter how to build a watch, when all he was asked was the time of day.

At the same time, if you don't know the answer to a

MEET THE PRESS

question, don't fake it. There's nothing shameful about saying: "I don't know but I'll find out and let you know." Such an answer, when followed up, gains the respect of the media.

In all, the person conducting the press conference or interview has an obligation to tell the truth, even if it becomes uncomfortable. He must remember that he is a public official, paid from public funds, entrusted with the operation of public schools. His activities are in the public domain and cannot be hidden under self-contrived cloaks of secrecy.

The school official who is honest with the news media can expect its respect and consideration. A newsman, like the school official, has a job to do. He wants to do it in the best and most professional manner. He is not out to get the public official he interviews, only to get facts.

Eschew Obfuscation

In preparing news releases, and in personal contact with the media, such as at press conferences, in briefings, and in giving speeches, speak English.

One of the ills of our modern society – and most particularly the bureaucracy – is that of not wanting to call a spade a spade or of relying on cliches to express oneself. In fact, it seems to please us far more if we can pass off the "spade" as a "long-handled agricultural implement utilized for the purpose of dislodging the earth's crust."

People no longer wish to be referred to in terms of yore; rather, the undertaker prefers to be called a funeral director, janitors are now maintenance engineers, housewives have become homemakers, and the list goes on.

This sort of euphemism can go to the most ridiculous of extremes, as witnessed in post-war Germany when the U.S. Army of Occupation was obliged to let some of its indigenous (local) help go. Letters of recommendation were written for the base cleaning women, upon whose heads the budgetary ax had fallen. To ease the pain of

PUBLIC RELATIONS

being let go, the letters were most flowery and praiseworthy. However, no sooner had the ladies received their commendatory letters than they were marching in protest on the personnel office. They demanded that their occupation of Putzfrau (cleaning woman) be changed to the more high-toned term: Verschoenerungsfrau (beautification lady). The malady transcends national boundaries as well as social classes.

Every occupation has its in-house terminology, some quite professional, some slangy, but all understandable primarily to those within the fraternity.

It's probably a close toss-up between the education and the military communities as to who prefers the greatest amount of latitude with respect to its abuses of the English language.

Words the military don't care for are either ignored altogether, or are replaced with more flattering or acceptable words, or obtuse phrases are substituted – often to the extent that they become everyday words and the user becomes a part of the farce himself.

In Cambodia, during the hot days of U.S. involvement – notice the reluctance to call it a war – a military press officer was berating newsmen. "You always write it's bombing, bombing, bombing. It's not bombing," he explained, "it's air support."

And even "bombing" was later spruced up and called "routine limited duration protective reaction strikes." And if the bombardiers missed the target, it became a "navigational misdirection."

Targeting during this military action was another matter. The Air Force could hardly take pride in destroying the grass huts of the hapless natives, therefore they became "suspected enemy structures." And when pilots fired on junks and sampans, reports had them shooting at "water borne logistics craft."

At the other end of the extreme, the military became so sensitive about certain subjects that the word "napalm" never appeared in military newspapers, nor were any

MEET THE PRESS

stories ever written about servicemen being ambushed by the enemy. All as if to convince oneself that "if we don't say it, it didn't happen."

In normal conversation, military people frequently answer questions in the "affirmative," or "negative," but seldom with a simple "yes" or "no."

Educators are little different in their approach to conversational English. They use so many terms, cliches and euphemisms that outsiders are constantly confused when attempting to make sense out of their conversation.

Take the case of a confused editorial writer who had interviewed a county school superintendent. After their talk he found that there was a category of student that he didn't understand. He asked the education reporter for clarification. "I believe I know what 875 children are, I know about Title I students, but what are 823 children?"

The reporter, too, was confused, but asked for clarification from the superintendent.

"Oh," said the educator, "they're regular students who come to school at 8 and stay to 3."

To further confound comprehension, educational jargon has been dressed up to the point where the jargon has become "communicative skills."

The mother who volunteers to help out at the local schoolhouse is either a "paraprofessional" or, if she lends a little more than help, a "resource person."

The toys, blocks and other playthings the little nippers amuse themselves with are "manipulatives," and the schoolmarm has a choice of calling herself a "facilitator," or a "change agent."

Sometimes these "facilitators" get their heads together and become a "task force." The conclusions they arrive at are "feedback," and when they get ready to put it all together it goes through a process called — if you will — "prioritizing." For shame.

Move down the hall at P.S. 3 and you might enter the "learning resources center," which resembles what we knew as a library. On the shelves and tables therein are "instructional system components." At this point we can

PUBLIC RELATIONS

imagine that some of the "resource center facilitator's" charges might be whispering among themselves, which might elicit the admonition: "Cease covert communication!"

And should some stern grammarian refuse to permit his students to speak in the vernacular, that person might well be accused of committing "linguistic apartheid."

All of which leads one to concur with Professor Scott Cutlip, who observes that:

> A cardinal premise is that you cannot tell anyone something he cannot understand. And you rarely can tell anyone something you cannot understand. You have to understand it first and then you have to make it understandable to the other person.

Say what you mean so that others can understand you. GIVE, don't CONTRIBUTE.

TRUTH is a far better word for the purpose of communication than VERACITY. BIG is quite sufficient. Leave MONUMENTAL or COLOSSAL to the movie flacks.

Be AFRAID, not APPREHENSIVE, of using words that you, or others, might not understand.

To sum all this concisely, we might say that simplicity is the mother of comprehension.

Mechanics of Press Conferences

Whenever possible, separate press conferences should be arranged for the broadcast and print media. They should be timed so as not to favor one over the other, but so as to provide the fullest service to each.

If facts and figures are to be presented, have copies available for the media representatives. The best way to insure that the correct information is read and heard is to have it available in writing.

Since broadcast newsmen have a certain amount of equipment indigenous to their trade, they need time to set up and prepare for the conference. Television crews need

MEET THE PRESS

lights and often wish to move about the room to obtain different photographic angles. Sufficient electrical outlets should be available, as well as tables for recording equipment.

The newspaper and wire service representative is content with his pencil and tablet – and perhaps, a tape recorder – and is easily attended to. He resents having to strain to hear the speaker over the sound of grinding television cameras, and further, he does not take kindly to cameramen jumping up in front of him while he's attempting to gather information.

In addition, some print media people complain that while they plan for news conferences, do prior research and prepare their questions, television and radio reporters often take advantage of this knowledge and ride free on the newspaperman's industry. Some publishers have even forbade their reporters from asking questions at a televised news conference for this very reason.

What often occurs is that a newspaperman will "scoop" himself by asking a pertinent question, only to have it on the six o'clock news that evening while his report would not appear until the following morning.

Practitioners should see that all segments of the media are equally attended to and that none receives consideration over the other.

Chapter VI

PHOTO COVERAGE

At times situations may arise where a news event may be supplemented with a photograph, or photographs. While a picture may be better than a thousand words, poor pictures, or pictures that say nothing, are not worth the time to take them.

Being humans, we like to see our pictures in the paper. However, are we denying the public the information that competent reporting of an event might provide in order that some executive's picture may fill the same space in the newspaper?

Practitioners should be selective in their efforts to provide photographic coverage. If the event calls for a photograph, then one should be taken. But using photos simply because a picture had been taken is a waste of both time and space.

Assuming that photographic coverage is in order, there are a few cautions that should be heeded. The first of these is: The possession of a camera does not necessarily mean that one is a photographer. If it is necessary to provide a photograph with a news release, seek professional help. Amateur snapshots and Polaroid photographs do not, as a rule, reproduce well in a newspaper.

If a newspaper sends a photographer to cover an event, the school representative should be prepared to assist, but should avoid attempting to give the photographer instructions.

In preparing for the arrival of the photographer, it is best not to convey the idea to those involved that they will all be in the picture. Don't try to set something up in advance. Let the professional select his subjects and setting. He knows what he is doing.

Normally he will want odd numbers of subjects for the picture; generally three or five. For daily papers it is best to keep the number of subjects to a minimum. Remember that each person in the picture must be identified in the caption. The more people, the more names. For weeklies, the reverse is true. Publishers of weekly newspapers

PUBLIC RELATIONS

generally tend to want large group shots.

If the subjects of the photograph are to be involved in some sort of endeavor, have necessary props handy. However, let the photographer set them up.

Don't concern yourself with background. Too much clutter tends to distract from the picture.

Advise the subjects to cooperate with the photographer. If it is a group picture, he will want them close together. People often feel uncomfortable when pressed together. But when the photograph is reproduced, this tight grouping results in a better picture.

Caution subjects against looking into the lens of the camera. Remind them that the photographer will tell them where he wants them to look, and that they should comply with his instructions.

Be prepared to provide names and titles of adults. If children are in the picture, have their full names, ages, addresses, and parents' names on hand, but no nicknames.

If the photographer arranges a grouping that includes members of only one race, it is not for ulterior reasons, rather for technical purposes. Because of skin tones and light absorption, mixed groups present difficulties that are eliminated by using subjects of one race. If this is not possible or practical, the photographer will understand and do the best he can.

In all, good photographs of people in action are a welcome addition to most stories. However, they are seldom substitutes for a well-written account of an event.

Photographs of people shaking hands, standing stiffly with a plaque in their hands, cutting ribbons, passing a check from one person to another, or poking a shovel into the ground, are both trite and are generally unacceptable at most newspapers.

If a picture will enhance the story, by all means use one, or however many are necessary. Don't waste time and money on pictures that serve no purpose other than having a photograph of the superintendent or some local dignitary looking at a piece of paper.[1]

Chapter VII

SUMMARY AND CONCLUSIONS

In all, public relations consists of a multitude of little chores, and a few big ones. What much of what we like to call public relations boils down to is common sense, courtesy, doing unto others as we would like them to do unto us.[1] But most importantly, it is doing these things in an honest and straightforward manner.

This is what the public expects from its educators: factual and honest explanations of what they are doing with the tax dollars provided them.[2]

If the public is to be expected to support its schools, it must know what their needs are. It wants facts, not generalities.[3]

Unfortunately, the public — through the news media — finds itself unable to pry such information out of many school people, especially if there is the slightest air of controversy about it.[4]

For reasons known only unto the education community, it appears to fear the public, and especially the inquiring reporter. It feels uneasy when asked to explain what it is doing with the money it has been provided, and frequently becomes hostile when its shortcomings are reported.[5] Yet, it has little or no reason for feeling this way.

The public wants, and should receive, the truth. No embellishments, just the facts — stated in plain, simple, easy to understand terms. Both the general public, as well as the internal public — teachers, professional staff, students, and parents — want to know what's going on; what the system is doing; what it would like to do; what it can't do; and the reasons therefor.[6]

A school system does not need a high-priced public relations practitioner on its staff. Such a person would be an asset, but is not essential to a successful public relations program. What is essential is a dedication on the part of the school board and the superintendent to a sound public relations policy, a workable public relations plan — based upon positive two-way communication — and a willingness

PUBLIC RELATIONS

to follow the plan once it has been formulated.

Every school system can enjoy amicable relations with its community if it is open and honest. The community will support the system if it knows that system is doing the best it can, is spending its resources wisely, and is willing to seek and accept the advice of the community.

Good public relations is nothing more than good common sense.

APPENDIX

Definition of Terms

Advance release – An item given to the media in advance of the date when it is permissible to be used.

Beat reporter – One who is assigned a particular area for coverage, such as education, courts, police.

Central office – The office of the local city or county superintendent of education.

Cub reporter – A new, inexperienced reporter.

Deadline – A set time by which a particular phase of publication or airing must be completed.

Editor – The person who supervises all phases, or a phase of planning, writing, revision, and publication of a newspaper, magazine or book.

External audience – The general public, as opposed to employees and staff, which constitute the "internal audience."

Five W's – The elements of news information: Who, What, When, Where, and Why. How is generally added.

General assignment reporter – One who is not assigned a particular beat, but covers any event, as assigned by his editor.

Hack – A derogatory term applied to less than qualified public relations practitioners and writers.

Handout – Story furnished free of charge to editors by individuals or organizations seeking publicity. (See also press release.)

Hard news – Legitimate news items, as opposed to events staged merely for publicity purposes.

Information person – Another term used to designate the person responsible for what may be generally considered the public relations program of an institution.

Information specialist – Title often given to an organization's public relations practitioner.

Internal audience – The members of an organization, employees, officers, staff.

News director – The person on the radio or television station staff in charge of the overall news production.

News media – Term used to refer to all segments such

as newspapers, radio, television, and news magazines.

News release — (See press release).

Off the record — Information provided by an individual in a responsible position which is either not to be used directly or, if used, without direct attribution.

Press — Term generally used to refer to the print media, but often applied to all segments of the news media.

Press agent — One entrusted with the responsibility of publicizing the activities of his employer.

Press release — An announcement of a timely and newsworthy event sent to the various media containing pertinent data (see Five W's above) from which a news story may be written.

Public relations (also public information, PR, community relations, public affairs, information, and a host of other pseudonyms) — According to Professor Scott Cutlip, "The planned effort to influence opinion through socially responsible and acceptable performance, based on mutually satisfactory two-way communication."

Public relations practitioner (or person) — That person entrusted with the responsibility for the public relations program.

Publicity puff — An item manufactured by a publicity agent of little news value, used primarily to obtain exposure for the organization or a particular individual.

Pyramiding — Practice of arranging contents of news story so that facts are related in order of their importance, most important first.

Style — That manner of presenting news employed by individual news agencies.

SELECTED BIBLIOGRAPHY

Adams, Alexander B. *Handbook of Practical Public Relations.* New York: Thomas Y. Crowell Co., 1965.

Ayer, N. W. *Ayer's Directory of Publications.* Philadelphia, Pa.: Ayer Press, 1975.

Charnley; Mitchell V. *Reporting.* New York: Holt, Rinehart and Winston, 1964.

Cutlip, Scott, and Center, Allen H. *Effective Public Relations,* 4th ed. Englewood Cliffs, N.J.: Prentice-Hall, Inc., 1971.

Hohenberg, John. *The Professional Journalist: A Guide to Modern Reporting Practice,* 1962 printing. New York: Holt, Rinehart and Winston, 1962.

Jones, James R. *School Public Relations.* New York: Center for Applied Research in Education, Inc., 1966.

Kindred, Leslie W. *How To Tell the School Story.* Englewood Cliffs, N.J.: Prentice-Hall, Inc., 1960.

Roalman, Arthur R. *Profitable Public Relations.* Homewood, Ill.: Dow Jones-Irwin, Inc., 1968.

Westley, Bruce. *News Editing.* Cambridge Mass.: Houghton Mifflin Co., 1953.

Lance, Carroll G. *Educators Meet the Press: A Communication Gap at the State Capital.* Madison, Wisc.: U.S. Office of Education, Project Public Information, 1968.

Sabine, Gordon. *Teachers Tell It – Like It Is, Like It Should Be.* Iowa City, Iowa: American College Testing Program Special Report Three, 1971.

Defense Information School. *Applied Journalism.* Fort Slocum, N.Y., 1964.

Defense Information School. *Broadcast Writing Style Guide.* Fort Benjamin Harrison, Ind., 1973.

Defense Information School. *Journalism Handbook.* Fort Benjamin Harrison, Ind., 1965.

Alabama State Department of Education. *SDE Report,* Vol. 3, No. 1, January 1971.

South Central Bell Telephone Co. *Alabama News Media Telephone Directory,* 31 March 1975.

Danilov, Victor J. "Business Editors List PR Likes and Dislikes." *Editor and Publisher,* 14 September 1957, p. 62.

Halperin, Samuel. "Politicians and Educators: Two World Views." *Phi Delta Kappan,* Vol. LVI, No. 3, November 1974, pp. 189-190.

Bitter, John. "The Communication Gap Between Educators and the Media." Master's Thesis, Troy State University, 1975.

Dean, Norman. President, Service Photography, Montgomery, Alabama. Interview, 24 October 1975.

Kimbrough, W. H. Director, Finance and Administration, Alabama State Department of Education. Interview, 5 December 1974.

NOTES

Chapter I

[1]See Carroll G. Lance, *Educators Meet the Press: A Communication Gap at the State Capital* (Madison, Wisc.: U. S. Office of Education, Project Information, 1968), p. 12; and Scott Cutlip and Allen H. Center, *Effective Public Relations,* 4th ed., (Englewood Cliffs, N. J.: Prentice-Hall, Inc. 1971), p. 561.

[2]Samuel Halperin, "Politicians and Educators: Two World Views," *Phi Delta Kappan,* Vol. LVI, No. 3, November 1974, p. 190.

[3]Cutlip, *Effective Public Relations,* p. 570.

[4]Lance, *Educators Meet Press,* p. 12.

[5]Cutlip, *Effective Public Relations,* p. 570.

[6]Leslie W. Kindred, *How To Tell The School Story,* (Englewood Cliffs, N.J.: Prentice-Hall, Inc., 1960), pp. 55-57.

[7]Lance, *Educators Meet Press,* p. 45.

[8]James Jones, *School Public Relations,* (New York: Center for Applied Research in Education, Inc., 1966), pp. 4-5.

[9]Gordon Sabine, *Teachers Tell It – Like It Is, Like It Should Be* (Iowa City: American College Testing Program, 1971), p. 77.

[10]Jones, *School Public Relations,* p. 6.

[11]John Bitter, "The Communication Gap Between Educators and the Media" (Master's thesis, Troy State University, 1975), p. 75.

[12]Ibid., p. 66.

[13]Jones, *School Public Relations,* pp. 46-49.

[14]Interview with W. H. Kimbrough, director of Finance and Administration, Alabama State Department of Education, 5 December 1974.

Chapter II

[1]Jones, *School Public Relations,* pp. 61-63.

[2]Cutlip, *Effective Public Relations,* p. 2.

[3]Jones, *School Public Relations,* pp. 106-7.

[4]Cutlip, *Effective Public Relations,* p. 572.

[5]Lance, *Educators Meet Press,* p. 30.

[6]Jones, *School Public Relations,* pp. 47-49.

Chapter III

[1]Cutlip, *Effective Public Relations,* p. 574.

[2]Jones, *School Public Relations,* p. 63.

[3]South Central Bell Telephone Co., *Alabama News Media Telephone Directory,* 31 March 1975.

[4]*Ayer's Directory of Publications* (Philadelphia, Pa.: Ayer Press, 1975), p. 111.

Chapter IV

[1]Kindred, *How To Tell School Story,* pp. 54-55.

[2] John A. Hohenberg, *The Professional Journalist: A Guide To Modern Reporting Practice* (New York: Holt, Rinehart and Winston, 1962 printing), p. 240.

[3] Victor J. Danilov, "Business Editors List PR Dislikes," *Editor and Publisher,* 14 September 1957, p. 6.

[4] Lance, *Educators Meet Press,* p. 45.

[5] Bruce Westley, *News Editing* (Cambridge, Mass.: Houghton Mifflin Co., 1953), p. 333.

[6] Hohenberg, *The Professional Journalist,* pp. 63-64.

[7] Mitchell V. Charnley, *Reporting* (New York: Holt, Rinehart and Winston, 1964), p. 34.

[8] Ibid., pp. 1-2.

[9] Hohenberg, *The Professional Journalist,* pp. 63-64

[10] Alexander B. Adams, *Handbook of Practical Public Relations* (New York: Thomas Y. Crowell Co., 1965), p. 35.

[11] Kindred, *How To Tell School Story,* pp. 55-57.

[12] See Arthur R. Roalman, *Profitable Public Relations* (Homewood, Ill.: Dow Jones-Irwin, Inc., 1968), pp. 29-31; and Adams, *Handbook,* p. 45.

[13] Hohenberg, *The Professional Journalist,* p. 243.

[14] Adams, *Handbook,* pp. 47-48.

[15] Kindred, *How To Tell School Story,* pp. 61-62.

[16]Adams, *Handbook,* p. 35.

[17]Ibid., p. 49.

[18]Lance, *Educators Meet Press,* p. 27.

[19]Kindred, *How To Tell School Story,* pp. 61-62.

[20]Hohenberg, *The Professional Journalist,* p. 225.

[21]*Applied Journalism* (Fort Slocum, N.Y.: The Defense Information School, 1964), pp. 14-15.

[22]*Applied Journalism Handbook* (Fort Benjamin Harrison, Ind.: The Defense Information School, 1965), pp. 22-23.

[23]Adams, *Handbook,* pp. 44-45.

[24]Hohenberg, *The Professional Journalist,* p. 240.

[25]Adams, *Handbook,* pp. 20-26.

[26]*Broadcast Writing Style Guide* (Fort Benjamin Harrison, Ind.: The Defense Information School, 1973), pp. 1-20.

Chapter VI

[1]Interview with Norman Dean, president of Service Photography, Montgomery, Alabama, 24 October 1975.

Chapter VII

[1]Cutlip, *Effective Public Relations,* p. 11.

[2]State Department of Education Report, "State News Media Voice Strong Comment on Educator Cooperation," January 1971, p. 4.

[3] Halperin, *Phi Delta Kappan,* p. 190.

[4] Lance, *Educators Meet Press,* p. 35.

[5] Halperin, *Phi Delta Kappan,* p. 190.

[6] Sabine, *Teachers Tell It,* p. 79.

INDEX

Accuracy, 12
Administrators, 1, 3, 4, 5
Advertiser, The, 3, 8
Adams, Alexander B., 12, 53, 54
Alabama, State Department of Education, 54
Associated Press, 8, 13, 22
Audience, 7, 8, 19
Audience, External, 7, 8
Audience, Internal, 7
Ayer, N. W., 9, 52

Background, 44
Birmingham Schools, 3
Bitter, John, 51
Bleyer, Willard G., 11
Brief, 18
Broadcast, 13, 19, 31, 32, 33, 40
Broadcaster, 9, 13, 31
Broadcast Release, 31, 32, 33

Central Office, 2, 3, 5, 13, 26, 47
Charnley, Mitchell V., 12, 53
City Editor, 13
Clark, Thomas, 11
Clear, 18
Coherent, 18
Communication, 1, 2, 3, 5, 7, 8, 45, 51
Community, 2, 3, 5, 6, 7, 12, 26, 46
Community Relations, 6
Conflict, 17

Consequence, 17
Cutlip, Scott, 51, 52, 54

Danilov, Victor J., 53
Dateline, 19
Deadline, 11, 14, 47
Dean, Norman, 54
Defense Information School, 54

Editor, 9, 11, 13, 19, 20, 26, 47
Education, 1, 5, 11, 13, 18, 45
Educator, 1, 2, 13, 36, 45
Elements of News, 17-18
Embargo, 15, 19
Emotion, 17
Emphasis, 18
English, 20, 36
Exclusive, 15
Explanation, 12

Facts, 2, 3, 11, 12, 14, 25, 27, 35, 36, 37, 40, 45
Fact Sheet, 16
Federal, 2, 13, 27
Five W's, 22, 24, 27, 47

Halperin, Samuel, 51, 55
Hohenberg, John, 53, 54
Huntsville, 3

Immediacy, 17
Information, 1, 4, 5, 7, 14, 15, 16, 19, 22, 25, 26, 27, 28, 45, 47
Interest, 12, 17
Interviews, 35-37

Inverted Pyramid, 25

Jefferson County, 3
Jones, James, 51, 52,

Kindred, Leslie W., 19, 51, 52, 53,
Kimbrough, W. H., 52

Lance, Carroll G., 51, 52, 53, 54, 55
Legislators, 1
Legislature, 35

Mobile, 3
Montgomery, 8

National Merit Scholarship Foundation, 15
News, 1, 2, 4, 11-13, 14, 15, 16, 17, 18, 19, 20, 22, 27, 32, 33, 35, 41, 43
News Director, 13, 34, 47
News Media, 2, 3, 4, 5, 8, 12-16, 17, 19, 20, 26, 33, 35, 37, 40, 41, 45, 47, 52
Newsmen, 2, 3, 4, 11, 12, 13, 14, 15, 16, 20, 35, 37, 40, 41
Newspapers, 1, 7, 8, 13, 14, 16, 19, 20, 22, 26, 27, 31, 41, 43,
News Release, 7, 8, 13, 15, 16, 17-20, 21, 23, 22, 25, 26, 27, 31, 43, 48
News Writing, 20, 22, 27, 33

Newsworthy, 2, 11, 12, 17, 26

Objective, 18
Oddity, 17
Off The Record, 15, 36, 48

Parents, 2, 5, 9
Photograph, 16, 43, 44,
Photographer, 43-44
Politics, 1
Press, 11, 16, 17, 35, 36, 48
Press Agentry, 17
Press Conference, 35-41
Press Release, 13, 19, 22, 31
Principals, 4, 26
Progress, 18
Prominence, 17
Proximity, 17
Public, 1, 2, 3, 4, 5, 7, 8, 17, 19, 37, 43, 45,
Public Education, 1, 4, 6, 31
Public Educator, 1
Publicity, 18, 48
Public Opinion, 7
Public Relations, 1, 4, 5, 6, 7, 11, 13, 15, 20, 26, 45, 46, 48
Public Relations Practitioner, 3, 5, 7, 8, 9, 11, 12, 13, 14, 15, 16, 17, 18, 19, 20, 22, 25, 27, 31, 32, 34, 41, 43, 45, 48

Radio, 1, 8, 13, 41
Release Date, 19
Reporter, 13, 14, 15-16, 22, 36, 41, 45
Roalman, Arthur R. 53

Sabine, Gordon, 49, 51, 55
Schools, 1, 2, 3, 4, 5, 6, 7, 8, 13, 14, 17, 18, 20, 22, 25, 26, 27, 31, 33, 35, 37, 43, 45, 46
School Boards, 5, 6, 7, 26, 32, 45
Sex, 17
Shotgunning, 15
South Central Bell, 52
Spencer, Lyle M., 12
Spokesman, 5, 7, 15, 35, 36
Superintendents, 2, 5, 6, 7, 12, 17, 26, 27, 31, 33, 35, 44, 45
Suspense, 18

Taxes, 4, 5
Teachers, 1, 2, 4, 7, 20, 31, 32, 45,
Television, 1, 8, 13, 40, 41
Timeliness, 12

United Press International, 8, 13
Unify, 18

Wire Services, 13, 31, 41
Westley, Bruce, 53